ILEOSTOMY DI PREPARATION GUIDE

Diet for Everyday Living

A Complete List Of Delicious Meals You Must Eat, Their Ingredients And Foods You Need To Stop Eating For A Healthy Life

Dr. Julia Brianna

Table of Contents

Chapter One 3
    Introduction 3
    Understanding Ileostomy 3
    Nutritional Needs Following Ileostomy Surgery 4
    Importance of Diet in Ileostomy Management 4
    20 Cooking Tricks For Ileostomy Patients 5

Chapter Two 8
    List of foods to eat with preparation procedures 8
    List of foods to avoid with an ileostomy 12

Chapter Three 17
    Precautions For Meal Preparation 17
    Healthy Eating Habits For Ileostomy Patients 18
    Meal Planning For Ileostomy Patients 19
    Balanced Diet Plans For Ileostomy Patients 19
    Ileostomy Friendly Recipes 20

Chapter Four 23
    Snack Ideas For Ileostomy Patients 23
    Hydration And Fluid Intake For Patients With Ileostomy .. 24
    List Of Ten Vitamins And Supplements For Ileostomy 25
    Managing Weight With Ileostomy 28

Chapter Five 30
    Eating Out With An Ileostomy 30
    Special Occasions And Ileostomy Diet 31

List Of Exercises For Ileostomy 33

Chapter Six 36

Mental Health And Ileostomy Diet 36

Support Networks For Ileostomy Patients 36

Coping With The Challenges Of Ileostomy Diet 37

Traveling With An Ileostomy 38

Transitioning To Solid Foods Following Ileostomy 40

Chapter Seven 41

Often-Asked Questions And Answers Regarding Managing Ileostomy Surgery 41

Maintaining A Healthy Gut Flora On An Ileostomy Diet 43

Mindful Eating Strategies For Ileostomy Patients 44

Managing Food Allergies And Sensitivity With An Ileostomy 45

Understanding Nutrient Absorption Via An Ileostomy 47

Chapter Eight 50

Changing Portion Sizes For Ileostomy Patients 50

Meal Preparation Methods And Procedures 50

Adding Fiber To An Ileostomy Diet 54

Cooking For A Family With An Ileostomy 55

Socialization And Ileostomy Diet 57

Conclusion 59

Author Appreciation 59

Chapter One

Introduction

Living with an ileostomy may be a major adjustment, affecting many parts of everyday life, including eating habits. Individuals who have had ileostomy surgery must often monitor their nutritional intake to promote recovery, avoid problems, and maintain general health.

This page discusses ileostomy, nutritional requirements after surgery, the role of diet in treatment, a list of suggested foods and preparation processes, foods to avoid, meal preparation precautions, and good eating habits for ileostomy patients.

Understanding Ileostomy

An ileostomy is a surgical treatment that involves diverting the end of the small intestine through a hole in the abdominal wall, creating a stoma. This surgery is often used when the colon or rectum has been injured, diseased, or removed as a result of inflammatory bowel disease, colorectal cancer, or trauma. The stoma permits waste to escape the body via an external pouching system, bypassing the colon and rectum.

Nutritional Needs Following Ileostomy Surgery

Individuals who have ileostomy surgery may encounter alterations in digestion and absorption, which may lead to vitamin shortages and dehydration. As a result, meeting nutritional needs requires a well-balanced diet. Adequate hydration is required to compensate for increased fluid loss from the stoma. Furthermore, some nutrients, such as electrolytes, vitamins, and minerals, may need extra care to avoid shortages.

Importance of Diet in Ileostomy Management

Diet is critical to successfully maintaining an ileostomy. A well-planned diet may help control stool consistency, lower the risk of clogs and obstructions, decrease gas production, and improve overall gastrointestinal health. Furthermore, making optimal nutritional choices may improve comfort, eliminate smells, and increase mental health.

20 Cooking Tricks For Ileostomy Patients

1. To help digestion, simmer veggies until soft and thoroughly cooked.

2. Choose lean meats like chicken, fish, and tofu to reduce your fat consumption.

3. Experiment with herbs and spices to enhance taste without using high-fat sauces.

4. Include modest, regular meals throughout the day to avoid overwhelming the digestive system.

5. Keep a food journal to see which foods cause stomach troubles and alter your diet appropriately.

6. Chew thoroughly to help digestion and avoid stoma obstructions.

7. Drink fluids in between meals rather than with them to prevent having too much liquid enter the digestive system all at once.

8. To lower the fat content of meals, steam or bake them rather than fried.

9. Limit your consumption of high-fiber foods like nuts, seeds, and whole grains to prevent bowel obstructions.

10. To limit output, choose low-residue meals such as white rice, pasta, and well-cooked vegetables.

11. Consume soluble fiber sources such as oatmeal, applesauce, and bananas to help thicken your stool.

12. Be cautious of portion quantities to avoid overeating, which may worsen stomach issues.

13. Avoid carbonated drinks and chewing gum, which might cause gas production.

14. Consider taking digestive enzymes or probiotics to improve digestion and gut health.

15. Freeze leftovers for easy dinners on days when cooking seems overwhelming.

16. To make digestion simpler, purée meals using a food processor or blender.

17. To limit your fat consumption, go for low-fat dairy products like skim milk or yogurt.

18. Stay hydrated by drinking water throughout the day, aiming for at least eight glasses each day.

19. Read food labels carefully to avoid unexpected sources of added sugars, fats, and fiber.

20. To satisfy nutritional demands, consume nutrient-dense foods such as fruits, vegetables, lean meats, and whole grains.

Chapter Two

List of foods to eat with preparation procedures

1. Bananas are a fantastic option since they are easy to digest and contain little fiber. Peel and eat raw, or incorporate into smoothies for extra nutrients.

2. White Rice: Cook white rice completely before eating it alone or with cooked veggies for a light and digestible meal.

3. Boiled potatoes: Peel and cook till soft. Mash or eat them simply for energy.

4. For a moderate fruit alternative, use unsweetened applesauce. Eat it straight or as a topping for porridge or yogurt.

5. Grill or bake boneless, skinless chicken breasts until well cooked. Avoid using spices that might irritate the digestive tract.

6. Steamed fish fillets with minimum seasoning are a lean protein source that is easy on the stomach.

7. Cook scrambled eggs with minimum fat and spice. For a more balanced supper, serve with bread or boiled veggies.

8. Smooth Nut Butter: Choose smooth nut butter that does not include lumps or seeds. Spread over toast or serve as a dip for fruits.

9. Peeled and sliced cucumbers provide a pleasant and hydrated snack.

10. Yogurt: Choose plain, low-fat yogurt without additional sweeteners. For extra taste, add fresh fruits or honey.

11. Boiled Carrots: Cook carrots until cooked, then serve them simple or mashed.

12. Cooked Spinach: Steam or boil until wilted. Because of its high fiber content, it should be c

14. Tender Beef: Cook lean slices of beef until tender. Avoid making rough or fibrous cuts.

15. Peel, boil and mash sweet potatoes to make a healthful side dish.

16. Peeled and sliced peaches make for a soft and luscious fruit alternative.

17. Ripe avocados may be mashed and spread over toast or used as a salad garnish.

18. Cooked pasta: Cook until soft, then serve with a little sauce or olive oil.

19. Hard-boiled eggs may be consumed straight or sliced into salads.

20. Tofu: Add tofu to stir-fries or salads for a plant-based protein source.

21. Peanut Butter Smoothie: Combine smooth peanut butter, banana, and yogurt for a healthful and nourishing drink.

22. Steam asparagus until soft, then serve as a side dish or in salads.

23. Cottage Cheese: For protein, use low-fat cottage cheese. Add fruits or veggies for taste.

24. Peeled and sliced pears are a mild fruit alternative.

25. Boiled White Fish: Cook white fish fillets until done. Season gently and serve with rice or veggies.

26. Cream of Wheat: Combine cream of wheat with water or milk to make a warm and cozy meal.

27. Canned pumpkin puree is a fiber-rich option. Consume straight or mix into baked products.

28. Cooked zucchini: Steam or sauté until tender. Because of the fiber content, it is best to consume in moderation.

29. Ripe papaya: Before eating, remove the seeds and peel them. It may be eaten straight or mixed with fruit salads.

30. Soft cheeses, such as mozzarella or brie, are simpler to digest. Enjoy with crackers or sandwiches.

List of foods to avoid with an ileostomy

1. Raw veggies are difficult to digest and may create obstructions. Before eating veggies, ensure that they are completely cooked.

2. Whole grains, such as whole wheat bread or brown rice, are rich in fiber, which may cause increased stool production and discomfort.

3. Nuts and seeds: They are difficult to digest and might cause discomfort or obstructions. Choose smooth nut butter instead.

4. Tough Meats: Tough cuts of meat, such as steak or pork chops, take a lot of chewing and may be difficult to digest.

5. High-Fiber Fruits: Berries and citrus fruits, which have rough skins or seeds, might worsen digestive difficulties. Select soft, peeled fruits instead.

6. Spicy meals may irritate the digestive system and increase stool production. Avoid foods that are seasoned with spicy spices.

7. Carbonated drinks may produce gas and bloating, resulting in discomfort and even pouch leakage.

8. Alcohol dehydrates and irritates the digestive system. Reduce or avoid alcohol intake.

9. Caffeinated beverages, such as coffee or tea, have been shown to accelerate bowel motions and increase stool production.

10. High-fat meals, such as fried dishes or creamy sauces, might induce diarrhea or digestive problems.

11. Dried fruits have high fiber, which may induce gas or bloating. Choose fresh, peeled fruits instead.

12. Raw Salad Greens: These greens are heavy in fiber and may be tough to digest. Before eating greens, cook or steam them.

13. Popcorn kernels may be difficult to digest and may result in blockages. Avoid eating popcorn.

14. Tough-Skinned Fruits: Fruits with tough skins, such as apples and pears, may be difficult to digest. Peel the fruits before eating.

15. Spicy condiments, such as hot sauce or salsa, may irritate the digestive system. Choose milder choices instead.

16. Stringy Vegetables: Fibrous vegetables, such as celery or kale, may be difficult to digest. Cook the veggies until soft.

17. Coconut: Coconut is tough to digest and may cause stomach issues. Avoid eating coconut goods.

18. High-sugar foods might increase stool production and induce diarrhea. Choose low-sugar alternatives instead.

19. Citrus fruits are acidic, which may irritate the digestive system. Choose delicate, peeled fruits instead.

20. Raw onions and garlic may produce gas and bloating. Before eating onions and garlic, be sure you completely cook them.

21. Whole beans and legumes have a lot of fiber, which may induce gas or bloating. Choose canned or well-cooked beans.

22. Excessive dairy intake might result in lactose intolerance symptoms such as flatulence and diarrhea. Limit your dairy consumption.

23. Tough pasta, such as whole wheat or high-fiber kinds, may be difficult to digest. Choose soft pasta instead.

24. Meat substitutes, such as tofu steaks or tempeh, may be difficult to stomach. Choose softer options or cook fully.

25. Chewy Candy: Chewy sweets are difficult to digest and may create blockages. Avoid eating chewy candies.

26. High-Fiber Cereals: Fiber-rich cereals might induce increased stool production and stomach pain. Choose low-fiber alternatives instead.

27. Spicy pickles may irritate the digestive system, leading to increased stool production. Choose mild pickles, or avoid them completely.

28. Artificial sweeteners may induce gastrointestinal irritation and aggravate existing digestive difficulties. Select natural sweeteners instead.

29. Sugary beverages may increase stool production and lead to diarrhea. Choose water or unsweetened drinks.

30. High-protein bars sometimes include artificial additives, which may cause gastric distress. Select natural, low-fiber snacks instead.

Chapter Three

Precautions For Meal Preparation

1. Thorough Cooking: Cook meals thoroughly to make them simpler to digest.

2. Avoid Cross-Contamination: To reduce the risk of foodborne disease, keep raw and cooked foods separate.

3. Portion amounts: Be cautious of your portion amounts to prevent overeating, which may cause pain or digestive troubles.

4. cleanliness Practices: Maintain adequate cleanliness when preparing meals to prevent the risk of infection near the stoma site.

5. Chew your meal completely to promote digestion and avoid obstructions in the digestive system.

Healthy Eating Habits For Ileostomy Patients

1. Stay Hydrated: Drink lots of fluids throughout the day to avoid dehydration and keep electrolytes balanced.

2. Eat Small, Frequent Meals: To aid digestion and avoid overloading the digestive system, choose smaller, more frequent meals.

3. Aim for a balanced diet that includes lean proteins, complex carbs, healthy fats, and necessary vitamins and minerals.

4. Fiber Management: Gradually include fiber-rich foods into your diet and track their impact on stool consistency and frequency.

5. Weight, hydration status, and stoma output should be monitored regularly to establish nutritional sufficiency and alter the diet as needed.

Finally, treating an ileostomy requires careful consideration of food choices to promote maximum health and well-being. Individuals with an ileostomy may successfully manage their condition and enhance their quality of life by recognizing their nutritional requirements, making appropriate food choices, and establishing good eating habits.

Meal Planning For Ileostomy Patients

Meal planning is an important part of ileostomy patients' everyday lives, affecting their health, comfort, and general well-being. Living with an ileostomy requires a strategic approach to eating to control digestive difficulties, maintain a balanced diet, and stay hydrated. In this article, we will look at several meal-planning tactics and concerns for ileostomy patients.

Balanced Diet Plans For Ileostomy Patients

Maintaining a balanced diet is critical for ileostomy patients' general health and preventing nutritional deficits. A healthy diet should include a range of elements, such as protein, carbs, fats, vitamins, and minerals. However, some dietary adjustments may be required to accommodate the alterations in digestion produced by an ileostomy.

Ileostomy Friendly Recipes

1. Oatmeal with bananas and honey:

• Ingredients include rolled oats, ripe bananas, honey, water, or lactose-free milk.

2. Baked chicken with mashed sweet potatoes.

• Ingredients include chicken breast, sweet potatoes, olive oil, salt, and pepper.

3. Quinoa Salad With Grilled Vegetables

• Ingredients include quinoa, bell peppers, zucchini, cherry tomatoes, olive oil, and lemon juice.

4. Steamed fish and steamed vegetables:

• Ingredients include white fish fillets, mixed vegetables (carrots, broccoli, green beans), lemon slices, and herbs.

5. Smoothies containing protein powder:

- Ingredients include spinach, banana, Greek yogurt, protein powder, water, and lactose-free milk.

6. Egg Muffins With Spinach And Feta:

- Ingredients include eggs, spinach, feta cheese, salt, and pepper.

7. Vegetable Soup:

- Ingredients include mixed veggies (carrots, celery, potatoes), low-sodium vegetable broth, and herbs.

8. Baked apples with cinnamon:

- Ingredients: Apples, cinnamon, and honey (optional).

Adapting traditional recipes for ileostomy patients:

1. Use spaghetti squash instead of pasta in meals such as spaghetti Bolognese or carbonara.

2. Cauliflower Rice as a Low-Fiber Alternative: In stir-fries or rice-based meals, use cauliflower rice for regular rice.

3. Ground Turkey in Place of Beef: Opt for ground turkey instead of beef in dishes like tacos, chili, or meatballs for simpler digestion.

4. Mashed Cauliflower as a Potato Substitute: Mashed cauliflower is a lighter alternative to mashed potatoes, ideal for accompanying grilled meats or seafood.

5. Zucchini Noodles for Pasta: Instead of regular pasta, use zucchini noodles in pesto pasta or spaghetti marinara.

6. Tofu or Tempeh for Protein: Incorporate tofu or tempeh into stir-fries, salads, or sandwiches for a plant-based protein source.

7. Coconut Milk Instead of Dairy: For a lactose-free alternative, use coconut milk for dairy in curries, soups, and creamy sauces.

8. Gluten-Free Flour for Baking: For smoother digestion, use gluten-free flour mixes in recipes such as muffins, pancakes, and cookies.

Chapter Four

Snack Ideas For Ileostomy Patients

1. Rice Cakes with Peanut Butter:

• Provides energy and protein without adding weight.

2. Greek Yogurt with Honey:

• Offers probiotics and a sweet treat that's mild on the stomach.

3. Nut Butter with Banana Slices:

• Offers a balance of healthy fats and potassium.

4. Rice Crackers with Hummus:

• Provides a delicious crunch with fiber-rich chickpeas.

5. Cottage Cheese and Pineapple:

• Protein and vitamin supplement with a zesty twist.

6. Boiled eggs:

• Provides high-quality protein in a compact and portable format.

7. Fruit Smoothies With Protein Powder:

• Great for a fast snack or meal replacement, since it is both hydrating and nutritious.

8. Vegetable Sticks and Guacamole:

• A nutritious snack rich in vitamins and healthy fats.

Hydration And Fluid Intake For Patients With Ileostomy

Adequate hydration is critical for ileostomy patients to maintain electrolyte balance and avoid dehydration. Here are a few tips:

• Aim for 8-10 glasses of water each day, drinking moderately throughout the day instead of gulping big quantities all at once.

• Replace lost electrolytes with electrolyte-rich beverages, such as coconut water or sports drinks, particularly in hot weather or after exercise.

• Limit caffeinated and alcoholic drinks to prevent dehydration.

• Monitor stoma output and modify fluid intake as needed, particularly during sickness.

• Consume water-rich foods like cucumbers, melons, and oranges to increase hydration.

• Consult a certified dietitian with expertise in ileostomy meals to create a customized hydration strategy tailored to individual requirements and preferences.

Individuals with an ileostomy may improve their nutritional intake and general well-being by following these principles, including ileostomy-friendly recipes, altering old favorites, selecting appropriate snacks, and emphasizing water.

List Of Ten Vitamins And Supplements For Ileostomy Patients

Living with an ileostomy may provide unique problems, especially in terms of maintaining optimum nutrition. Following surgery, people may notice changes in their body's capacity to absorb critical vitamins and minerals.

As a result, ileostomy patients must supplement their diet with essential nutrients to promote overall health and wellness.

1. Multivitamin: A high-quality multivitamin designed for people with ileostomies may help cover nutritional shortages. Look for formulas that are particularly created for those with digestive disorders.

2. Vitamin B12: Patients with ileostomy may have trouble absorbing vitamin B12, which is necessary for nerve function and red blood cell synthesis. Sublingual or injectable versions of B12 are often prescribed.

3. Calcium: Because the ileostomy skips the large intestine, where calcium is predominantly absorbed, maintaining appropriate calcium levels is critical for bone health. Calcium supplements may assist in avoiding deficits.

4. Vitamin D: Vitamin D works in unison with calcium to help in calcium absorption and increase bone strength.

Many ileostomy patients need supplements to maintain appropriate levels.

5. Iron deficiency anemia may be a problem for ileostomy patients owing to reduced absorption. Iron supplements may be required to avoid tiredness and other symptoms caused by low iron levels.

6. Magnesium is essential for muscle and nerve functioning, as well as the health bones. Supplementation may be required to maintain appropriate levels, particularly if absorption is reduced.

7. Vitamin C: As a potent antioxidant, vitamin C promotes immune function and wound healing, which may be very helpful for ileostomy patients throughout the rehabilitation process.

8. Zinc supplementation, which is essential for immune function and wound healing, may be required for ileostomy patients, particularly if they have regular skin irritation around the stoma.

9. Omega-3 Fatty Acids: These beneficial fats are anti-inflammatory and promote cardiovascular health. Omega-3 supplements may improve general health in those who have an ileostomy.

10. Probiotics: A proper balance of gut bacteria is essential for digestion and immunological function. Probiotic supplements may assist in maintaining gut health, which may be damaged in certain ileostomy patients.

Managing Weight With Ileostomy

Individuals with an ileostomy may struggle with weight control due to changes in digestive function, which may affect appetite, nutrition absorption, and metabolism. Here are some ideas for good weight management:

1. Monitor Caloric Intake: Keep track of your daily caloric intake to ensure you're eating enough to be healthy. This may need changing portion sizes or increasing the frequency of meals and snacks.

2. Focus on Nutrient-Dense Foods: To promote general health, prioritize foods high in important vitamins, minerals, and protein. Your diet should be based on lean proteins, fruits and vegetables, entire grains, and healthy fats.

3. Stay Hydrated: Proper hydration is necessary for digestion and general health. Drink lots of fluids throughout the day, particularly water, to avoid dehydration, which may cause weariness and other health difficulties.

4. Exercise regularly may help you retain muscle mass, enhance metabolism, and control your weight. Aim for a balance of cardiovascular, strength, and flexibility workouts.

5. Seek Professional Help: If you're having trouble managing your weight or have particular dietary problems, speak with a registered dietitian or healthcare practitioner who can provide specialized advice and assistance.

Chapter Five

Eating Out With An Ileostomy

Dining out may be fun and stress-free for those who have an ileostomy with proper preparation and thoughtfulness. Here's some advice for handling restaurants and social gatherings:

1. Restaurant Research: Before going out to eat, do some research to identify restaurants that provide a range of alternatives for those with certain dietary requirements. Many places now provide menus online, making it easy to compare their offers.

2. Communicate with personnel: Don't be afraid to express your dietary limitations and preferences to restaurant personnel. They are often ready to fulfill unique requests or make changes to meals to meet your requirements.

3. Choose Wisely: Look for foods that are easy to digest and unlikely to cause pain or irritation. Avoid meals that

are extremely spicy, oily, or heavy in fiber, since these may aggravate digestive troubles.

4. Be Prepared: Bring any essential supplies, such as additional ostomy pouches or wipes, in case of an emergency. Having these things on hand may bring peace of mind and boost your confidence while eating out.

5. Enjoy Yourself: Remember that eating out should be a pleasant experience. Instead of worrying about your food limitations, focus on spending time with friends and family. With careful planning and preparation, you may still enjoy excellent meals and mingle with confidence.

Special Occasions And Ileostomy Diet

Food is typically central to special events and festivities, which may make eating difficult for people with ileostomies. However, with some careful planning and preparation, you may thoroughly enjoy these activities without sacrificing your nutritional demands.

1. Plan Ahead: If you know you'll be attending a special event, schedule your meals and snacks properly to ensure

you're well-nourished throughout the day. This might assist in avoiding overindulgence or feeling starved later on.

2. Bring Your Own: If you're not sure what food alternatives are available at the gathering, try bringing a dish or two that you know you can safely eat. This ensures that you'll have something to eat and lowers the likelihood of meeting trigger foods.

3. Communicate with Hosts: If you feel comfortable doing so, let the event hosts know about your dietary restrictions ahead of time. They may be willing to accommodate your requests or give further information about the menu.

4. Focus on Socializing: While eating is frequently an important part of special occasions, keep in mind that the primary objective of these gatherings is to celebrate and reconnect with loved ones. Turn your attention away from the buffet table and onto mingling and creating memories.

5. Practice Mindful Eating: If you decide to indulge in special sweets or meals, appreciate each mouthful and pay attention to your body's hunger and fullness signals. This may help you avoid overeating and have a more pleasurable dining experience.

List Of Exercises For Ileostomy

Individuals with an ileostomy benefit greatly from regular exercise as part of their general health and well-being. The following workouts are typically safe and beneficial:

1. Walking: Walking is a low-impact activity that you may simply add to your regular schedule. Aim for at least 30 minutes of brisk walking most days of the week to boost cardiovascular health and general fitness.

2. Swimming is a wonderful type of exercise for ileostomy patients since it is mild on the joints while yet providing a full-body workout. Just make sure you use a watertight ostomy pouch and take steps to avoid leakage.

3. Yoga is a blend of stretching, strengthening, and relaxation methods that improve both the body and mind. Look for yoga sessions or videos that are particularly developed for people with ostomies and may contain adaptations to meet your requirements.

4. Cycling: Cycling is another low-impact workout that may aid with cardiovascular fitness and leg strength. Invest in a comfortable bike seat and consider utilizing a stationary cycle if outside riding is not an option.

5. Strength Training: Including strength training activities, such as weightlifting or resistance band workouts, may help you retain muscle mass and bone density. Concentrate on activities that work key muscular groups, such as squats, lunges, and bicep curls.

6. Pilates emphasizes core strength, flexibility, and body awareness, making it a good alternative for ileostomy patients. Look for Pilates programs or DVDs that teach appropriate breathing methods and provide adaptations as required.

7. Tai Chi is a peaceful martial technique that blends slow, flowing motions, deep breathing, and meditation. It may increase balance, flexibility, and mental well-being, making it appropriate for people at all fitness levels.

8. Water Aerobics: Classes provide a fun and effective approach to working in a supportive setting. The buoyancy of the water lowers joint stress and provides a wider range of motion.

9. Stretching: Incorporate regular stretching exercises into your daily routine to increase flexibility and avoid muscular tightness. Stretch all main muscle groups, giving specific attention to places that feel tight or uncomfortable.

10. Balance Exercises: Performing balance exercises, such as standing on one leg or utilizing a balance board, may assist increase stability and lower the chance of falling. Begin cautiously, gradually increasing the challenge as your balance improves.

Chapter Six

Mental Health And Ileostomy Diet

Living with an ileostomy may bring several obstacles, particularly in terms of mental health and sticking to a specified eating plan. Individuals may, however, handle these problems more easily if they have strong support networks and appropriate coping techniques in place.

Furthermore, knowing how to manage an ileostomy diet while traveling is critical for sustaining physical and mental health.

Support Networks For Ileostomy Patients

Support networks are critical in assisting ileostomy patients in coping with the physical and mental changes associated with their disease. These networks may include healthcare professionals, support groups, internet forums, friends, and family members.

Healthcare specialists, such as ostomy care nurses or dietitians, may provide useful advice on how to manage the ileostomy diet and treat any nutritional and general health problems. Support groups and online communities provide a forum for people to interact with others who understand their experiences and may give empathy, support, and practical guidance.

Coping With The Challenges Of Ileostomy Diet

The ileostomy diet necessitates cautious food selection to avoid issues such as blockages, dehydration, and excessive output. Coping with the problems of this diet requires knowledge, experimentation, and adaptability. Patients often collaborate with healthcare providers to create individualized nutrition programs based on their unique requirements and preferences.

This might include progressively reintroducing items into their diet, monitoring how various meals influence their stoma output, and modifying their fiber, hydration, and vitamin intake appropriately. While some foods may need to be avoided or taken in moderation, there are still several alternatives for keeping a healthy and pleasurable diet.

Beyond nutritional issues, dealing with the complications of an ileostomy entails addressing emotional and psychological elements. Many people feel anxious, self-conscious, or depressed as a result of their disease. Seeking assistance from loved ones, mental health experts, or peer support groups may help people manage their emotions and build effective coping techniques.

Mindfulness, relaxation methods, and participating in activities that offer pleasure and satisfaction may all help to improve general well-being.

Traveling With An Ileostomy

Traveling with an ileostomy requires careful planning and preparation to guarantee a comfortable and pleasurable trip. Before going on a journey, people should check with their healthcare team to discuss any concerns and collect any required supplies, prescriptions, and documents.

It is critical to take additional ostomy supplies, including pouches, adhesive products, and cleaning materials, in case of unforeseen delays or crises. Researching places ahead of time might assist in identifying accessible restrooms and locating medical assistance if necessary.

Maintaining sufficient water and nourishment while traveling is critical for successfully managing an ileostomy. Individuals should plan meals and snacks that accommodate their dietary requirements, and consider carrying portable, non-perishable choices for times when fresh options are restricted. Staying hydrated is critical, especially in hot regions or during intense activity, to avoid dehydration and electrolyte imbalances.

To summarize, overcoming the obstacles of an ileostomy diet needs a mix of information, support, and adaptability. Individuals living with an ileostomy may improve their general well-being and quality of life by forming strong support networks, effective coping skills, and travel preparation.

Transitioning To Solid Foods Following Ileostomy Surgery

Transitioning to solid meals after ileostomy surgery is an important step in regaining a sense of normality and eating a healthy diet. However, it is critical to approach this change with caution and understanding of your body's requirements.

Chapter Seven

Often-Asked Questions And Answers Regarding Managing Ileostomy Surgery

Below are some often-asked questions regarding managing the world of solid meals after ileostomy surgery:

1. Which meals should I introduce initially following ileostomy surgery?

• Begin with readily digested meals, like cooked vegetables, ripe fruits without seeds or peel, lean meats like chicken or fish, and well-cooked grains like rice or oatmeal. These meals are mild on the digestive tract and may help you gradually resume eating solids.

2. How can I gently add fiber to my diet?

• While fiber is necessary for digestive health, adding it too rapidly might create pain or clogs. Begin with soluble fibers from meals such as oatmeal, bananas, and peeled apples. As your body adapts, gradually include insoluble fibers found in veggies, whole grains, and nuts.

3. Are there any foods I should completely avoid after ileostomy surgery?

• Certain foods might be problematic for ileostomy patients, notwithstanding individual tolerance levels. These include tough meats, nuts, seeds, popcorn, corn, raw vegetables, and fiber-rich foods such as broccoli and cabbage. It's best to start slowly and observe how your body reacts to different foods.

4. How can I make sure I'm getting enough nutrients on a limited diet?

• Choose nutrient-dense, easily digestible foods like lean proteins, cooked vegetables, and fruits. Consider consulting a dietitian who specializes in post-ileostomy nutrition to create a meal plan tailored to your specific requirements.

Maintaining A Healthy Gut Flora On An Ileostomy Diet

Maintaining a healthy gut flora is essential for overall digestive health, particularly for people who have an ileostomy. The strategies listed below can help support a thriving gut microbiome while living with an ileostomy.

1. Incorporate probiotic-rich foods: Probiotics are beneficial bacteria that improve gut health. Probiotic-rich foods like yogurt, kefir, kimchi, sauerkraut, and kombucha can help replenish and diversify your gut microbiota.

2. Choose prebiotic foods: Prebiotics are non-digestible fibers that provide fuel for probiotics, allowing them to thrive in the gut. Prebiotic-rich foods include garlic, onions, leeks, asparagus, bananas, and whole grains. Incorporating these foods into your diet can help to nourish good bacteria in your digestive system.

3. Stay hydrated: Proper hydration is critical for maintaining healthy digestion and promoting the growth

of beneficial gut bacteria. Drink plenty of water and herbal teas throughout the day to stay hydrated.

4. Limit your intake of processed foods and refined sugars, as they can disrupt gut bacteria balance and contribute to digestive tract inflammation. Choose whole, unprocessed foods whenever possible, and limit your consumption of sugary snacks and desserts.

Mindful Eating Strategies For Ileostomy Patients

Mindful eating entails paying complete attention to the experience of eating and drinking, both inside and outside of the body. For ileostomy patients, practicing mindfulness can help them enjoy their meals while also promoting digestion. Here are some mindful eating habits to consider:

1. Eat slowly and savor each bite: Take your time chewing your food thoroughly, paying attention to the texture, flavor, and aroma. Eating slowly can help with digestion and reduce post-meal discomfort or digestive issues.

2. Pay attention to your body's hunger and fullness cues, and eat only when you're truly hungry. Stop eating when you're full, even if you still have food on your plate.

3. Reduce distractions during meals: Turn off the TV, put away your phone, and concentrate solely on the experience of eating. Eliminating distractions allows you to completely engage your senses and absorb the nutrients provided by your meal.

4. Practice thankfulness for your meals: Develop an attitude of gratitude for the food on your plate and the nutrients it offers to your body. Taking a minute to notice the work that went into cooking your dinner will help you enjoy and appreciate it more.

Managing Food Allergies And Sensitivity With An Ileostomy

Managing food allergies and sensitivities may be difficult for anybody, but it is particularly crucial for those with an ileostomy. Here are some suggestions for managing food allergies and sensitivities while eating a nutritious diet:

1. Identify trigger foods: Keep a food journal to document your symptoms and look for trends or connections between certain foods and digestive problems. Dairy, gluten, nuts, seeds, and high-fiber meals are all potential triggers for ileostomy patients.

2. Experiment with elimination diets: If you feel that specific foods are causing allergy responses or sensitivities, try temporarily removing them from your diet to see if your symptoms improve. Reintroduce removed foods one at a time to determine particular triggers.

3. Read food labels carefully: Be aware of any allergies or additives that may cause stomach troubles. Look for hidden sources of common allergies like dairy, soy, and gluten, and use certified gluten-free or allergen-free items wherever feasible.

4. Work with a dietician: Speak with a qualified dietitian who specializes in food allergies and gastrointestinal health to create a personalized meal plan that fits your

nutritional requirements while avoiding trigger foods. A dietician can provide insight and support as you manage dietary allergies and sensitivities.

Understanding Nutrient Absorption Via An Ileostomy

An ileostomy might impact nutrient absorption because it affects the structure of the digestive system. Understanding how nutrient absorption works after ileostomy will help you make intelligent food choices that satisfy your body's nutritional requirements. Here are some important aspects to consider:

1. Reduced absorption of some nutrients: Following ileostomy surgery, the small intestine may have a shorter transit time, resulting in lower absorption of nutrients such as vitamin B12, iron, calcium, and magnesium. It is important to eat meals high in essential nutrients and, if required, take supplements as directed by your healthcare physician.

2. Adequate hydration is critical for good nutritional absorption, particularly for those who have an ileostomy.

Because fluid absorption occurs predominantly in the large intestine, which may be skipped or partly removed after surgery, it is critical to consume lots of fluids throughout the day to avoid dehydration and improve nutrient absorption.

3. Considerations for fat absorption: Some ileostomy patients may have difficulty absorbing fat, resulting in increased stool production or malabsorption of fat-soluble vitamins such as A, D, E, and K. Including healthy fats like avocados, nuts, seeds, and olive oil in your diet will aid with fat absorption and ensuring you receive enough nutrients.

4. Monitoring nutritional status: Regular monitoring of your nutritional condition, including blood tests and meetings with healthcare specialists, is critical for diagnosing any deficiencies or imbalances that may emerge post-ileostomy. Adjusting your diet and supplements program based on these results may help you improve nutrient absorption and general health.

In conclusion, adjusting to solid meals following ileostomy surgery requires patience, experimenting, and paying close attention to your body's demands. You may promote your digestive health and general well-being after an ileostomy by gently reintroducing meals, selecting nutrient-rich options, and adopting mindful eating habits.

Furthermore, controlling food allergies and sensitivities, keeping a healthy gut flora, and understanding nutrient absorption are all important concerns for optimizing your dietary approach and fulfilling your body's nutritional needs successfully. Working closely with healthcare experts, such as dietitians and doctors, may give invaluable direction and support as you strive for a balanced and nutritious diet with an ileostomy.

Chapter Eight

Changing Portion Sizes For Ileostomy Patients

Living with an ileostomy has unique problems, notably in terms of food and nutrition. Adjusting portion sizes is an important part of keeping people with ileostomies healthy and comfortable. Because the digestive system functions differently after surgery, it is critical to learn how to portion meals correctly to prevent pain, dehydration, and malnutrition. We will look at the complexity of portion management for ileostomy patients, including meal preparation, fiber inclusion, cooking for a family, socializing, and nutritional monitoring.

Meal Preparation Methods And Procedures

1. Marinate chicken breasts in olive oil, lemon juice, and herbs before grilling them with steamed vegetables. Grill till cooked through. Serve with steamed veggies like broccoli, carrots, and zucchini.

2. Season the salmon fillets with salt, pepper, and lemon zest. Serve over quinoa and roasted asparagus. Bake till flaky. Serve with cooked quinoa and roasted asparagus spears.

3. Turkey and Vegetable Stir-Fry: Sauté lean ground turkey with a variety of colorful veggies, including bell peppers, onions, and snap peas. Season with garlic, ginger, and low-sodium soy sauce. Serve with brown rice.

4. Vegetable Omelet: Whisk the eggs and pour them onto a heated pan. Include diced veggies like spinach, tomatoes, and mushrooms. Fold over and cook until set.

5. Shrimp Tacos: Saute shrimp in taco seasoning until pink and cooked through. Serve on corn tortillas with shredded lettuce, sliced tomatoes, and avocado slices.

6. Beef and Broccoli Stir-fried: Thinly slice beef and stir-fried with broccoli florets in a sauce made of soy sauce, garlic, and ginger. Serve with rice or noodles.

7. Grilled Veggie Panini: Cook sliced eggplant, zucchini, and red bell pepper. Spread pesto and mozzarella cheese over whole-grain bread. Press in a panini press until golden and crispy.

8. Mango Chicken Salad: Grill and slice chicken breasts. Toss in mixed greens, sliced mango, avocado, and a citrus vinaigrette dressing.

9. Lentil Soup: Cook onions, carrots, and celery until tender. Combine lentils, vegetable broth, and chopped tomatoes. Simmer until the lentils are soft. Season with herbs and spices.

10. Tuna Salad Lettuce Wraps: Combine canned tuna, Greek yogurt, sliced celery, and onions. Spoon into lettuce leaves and wrap up.

11. Baked Cod with Lemon and Herbs: Arrange cod fillets on a baking sheet. Drizzle with olive oil and lemon juice, then garnish with fresh herbs such as dill or parsley. Bake until the fish flaked easily with a fork.

12. Quinoa Stuffed Bell Peppers: Cook the quinoa according to the package directions. Combine black beans, corn, chopped tomatoes, and seasonings. Stuff half the bell peppers and bake until tender.

13. Chicken and Vegetable Skewers: Thread chicken breast, bell peppers, onions, and cherry tomatoes onto skewers. Grill until the chicken is fully cooked and the veggies are soft.

14. Eggplant Parmesan: Bread eggplant slices and bake till crispy. Layer with marinara and mozzarella cheese. Bake till bubbling and golden.

15. Greek Yogurt Parfait: For a healthy and filling snack or breakfast, layer Greek yogurt with fresh berries, oats, and a drizzle of honey.

16. Stuffed Portobello Mushrooms: Remove the stems from the portobello mushrooms and fill them with cooked quinoa, spinach, and feta cheese. Bake until the mushrooms are soft.

17. Asian Chicken Lettuce Wraps: Cook ground chicken with garlic, ginger, and hoisin sauce. Spoon onto lettuce leaves and serve with sliced green onions and chopped peanuts.

18. Black Bean and Corn Salad: Mix black beans, corn, chopped tomatoes, avocado, and cilantro. For a refreshing side dish, toss with lime juice and olive oil.

19. Sauté the onions, garlic, and bell peppers for the Sweet Potato and Black Bean Chili. Add the chopped sweet potatoes, black beans, tomatoes, and seasonings. Simmer until the sweet potatoes are soft.

20. Mediterranean Pasta Salad: Combine cooked whole wheat pasta, chopped cucumbers, cherry tomatoes, Kalamata olives, feta cheese, and a lemon-herb vinaigrette.

Adding Fiber To An Ileostomy Diet

Fiber is an important component that helps with digestion and supports intestinal regularity. However, patients with an ileostomy must approach fiber intake with care to avoid clogs or pain. Here are some ways to securely introduce fiber into your ileostomy diet:

• Introduce fiber-rich meals gradually to let your digestive system adapt. Start with modest amounts and gradually increase as acceptable.

• Soluble fiber sources include oats, barley, fruits (bananas and applesauce), and vegetables (cooked carrots and squash). Soluble fiber dissolves in water, making it less prone to create blockages.

• Limit or eliminate insoluble fiber sources, including raw fruits and vegetables, whole grains, nuts, and seeds, since they may be difficult to digest and increase the risk of obstruction.

• Stay Hydrated: Drink lots of fluids, particularly water, to soften stool and avoid dehydration, which is more prevalent in ileostomy patients.

Cooking For A Family With An Ileostomy

Cooking for a family with an ileostomy needs careful meal preparation and consideration of dietary limitations.

Here are some tips for cooking meals that are appropriate for both the person with an ileostomy and the rest of the family:

• Emphasize complete foods, including lean meats, fruits, vegetables, whole grains, and healthy fats. These meals are typically well-accepted and include necessary nutrients for everyone.

• Customize meals to meet individual tastes and dietary requirements. For example, provide sauces and toppings on the side so that each guest may adapt to their taste and tolerance.

• Adjust meal sizes for those with ileostomies while maintaining appropriate nourishment for other family members. To reduce pain for the person with an ileostomy, consider offering smaller servings of high-fiber or gas-producing meals.

• Encourage open conversation about food preferences and requirements among family members. Discuss any problems or difficulties with meal planning and develop solutions that work for everyone.

Socialization And Ileostomy Diet

Socializing may be pleasurable, but it can also be difficult for people with ileostomies, especially when it comes to eating out. Here are some guidelines for handling social events while maintaining an ileostomy diet:

• When attending social events or eating out, investigate menu alternatives and communicate any dietary limitations to the host or restaurant personnel.

• Bring your snacks or meals to social occasions to guarantee safe and appropriate selections.

• Be adaptable to diverse eating contexts. Look for basic, readily digestible alternatives on the menu, and don't be afraid to ask for changes if necessary.

• Educate friends and family about your dietary preferences and the problems of living with an ileostomy.

Increased awareness and understanding might result in more assistance and accommodation.

Monitoring nutrient levels with an ileostomy

Individuals with an ileostomy must monitor their nutrition levels to maintain optimum health and well-being. Here are some critical nutrients to concentrate on, along with guidelines for monitoring levels:

• Consume lean protein sources such as chicken, fish, eggs, tofu, and lentils. Monitor your protein intake to maintain proper healing and tissue repair.

• An ileostomy might cause electrolyte abnormalities owing to increased fluid loss. Stay hydrated and eat foods high in electrolytes, such as bananas, potatoes, yogurt, and coconut water.

• Monitor your vitamin and mineral consumption, especially vitamin B12, calcium, and iron, since these may be influenced by digestion. Consider taking supplements if required, and get advice from a healthcare expert.

Conclusion

Adjusting meal sizes for people with ileostomies is critical for maintaining good health and comfort. Individuals who understand the specific dietary demands and problems associated with living with an ileostomy may make more educated decisions regarding meal preparation, fiber inclusion, cooking for their family, socializing, and nutritional monitoring.

A diverse and healthy diet may be enjoyed while managing an ileostomy with careful planning, communication, and awareness.

Author Appreciation

I am grateful to the readers and families who have read this book and have known many facts about ileostomy care and nutrition. Your commitment and effort is very much appreciated.

Printed in Great Britain
by Amazon